Barrier Breakers

Ian Rohr

Published by
Sundance Publishing
P.O. Box 1326
234 Taylor Street
Littleton, MA 01460
800-343-8204
www.sundancepub.com

First published 2002 by
Blake Education, Locked Bag 2022, Glebe 2037, Australia
Exclusive United States Distribution: Sundance Publishing

Design by Cliff Watt in association with
Sundance Publishing

Barrier Breakers
ISBN 0-7608-6699-6

Photo Credits:
p. 1 and back cover (left) UWC-Robben Island Mayibuye Archives; back cover (right) Anders Hellengren; p. 9 (top) MEPL, (bottom) photolibrary.com; p. 10–11 MEPL; p. 13 APL/Corbis; p. 16 (bottom) MEPL; p. 17 (top) MEPL; p. 18 MEPL ; p. 19 (bottom) APL/Corbis; p. 20 photolibrary.com; p. 21 MEPL; pp. 24–25 UWC-Robben Island Mayibuye Archives; p. 26 (top) Anders Hellengren, (bottom) UWC-Robben Island Mayibuye Archives; p. 27 (bottom) Anders Hellengren; p. 28 APL/Corbis; p. 29 (top) APL/Corbis, (bottom) The Nobel Foundation.

Printed in Canada

Table of Contents

Nothing to
worry about.
Full speed ahead!

Sailing into the Unknown: Ferdinand Magellan

Imagine a daring plan to sail right around the world . . . with no maps to help you find the next piece of land.

Five hundred years ago, the people of Europe wanted the silks and spices from the East. The way east across land was long and lined with robbers. The only known sea route was also eastward, around the tip of Africa.

In 1492, Christopher Columbus set sail from Europe. He planned to discover the rich lands of Asia by sailing west into uncharted seas. Today we know that Columbus reached the Americas on that voyage. But he believed he had reached the East Indies.

Westward to Wealth

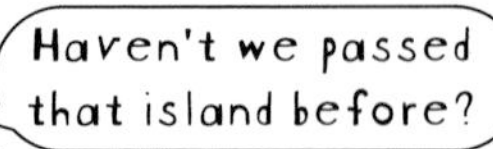

By 1517, an explorer named Ferdinand Magellan knew that Columbus was wrong. Another ocean lay on the west coast of the Americas. Could Magellan find a passage through the Americas to the riches of the East?

A Man with a Plan

Magellan knew that if he found a new route to the Spice Islands, he would gain instant wealth and fame. His plan was to sail west and find a sea passage from the Atlantic Ocean, through the Americas. He would then sail to the Spice Islands (part of present-day Indonesia).

Magellan was Portuguese, but he quarreled with the Portuguese king. He then asked King Charles of Spain to sponsor the voyage. The Spanish king supplied five old, leaky ships. At last, in 1519, Magellan was ready to sail. But he did not tell the crew his plan. They might **mutiny** if they knew what lay ahead!

Ferdinand Magellan (1480–1521)

The Known World in the late 1400s

In 1494, Spain and Portugal signed a treaty that gave all unclaimed lands west of the Atlantic to Spain. It gave all unclaimed lands east of the Atlantic to Portugal. By sailing west, Magellan believed he could prove that the Spice Islands were in Spain's half of the world.

Trading in Spices

There were no refrigerators to keep food fresh. Spices were added to food to make it last longer and to help disguise the taste of old meat. When they could get them, wealthy European women used spices to freshen their breath.

Rumblings at Sea

At first, things went well. The five ships reached what is now Rio de Janeiro and took on fresh food and water. Then they sailed down the coast of South America, looking for a sea passage to Asia. But they couldn't find one. Some of the Spanish sailors did not trust Magellan because he was Portuguese. Twice, the crews tried to mutiny. Magellan punished or **marooned,** or stranded, the leaders.

A Dangerous Passage

Finally, after more than a year and the wrecking of another ship, Magellan sighted a narrow opening near the southern tip of South America. But the **strait** was stormy and a maze of islands. It took 38 days to find a way through the strait. One ship turned and sailed back to Spain—with most of the food! At last, the three remaining ships entered a calm ocean. Magellan wept with joy and named it *Pacific,* which means "peaceful."

Magellan's flagship was called the *Victoria*, meaning "Victory."

Food and Supplies

- flour and salt to make bread
- hard, dry ship's biscuits
- dried fish
- meat preserved in saltwater
- salt pork
- barrels of fresh water
- barrels of wine

Some leaders of the mutiny were put in stocks (shown above). At least one man had his head cut off and his body cut into quarters.

An artist's rendition of Magellan's ships finding a way through the dangerous strait.

For Trade

- red velvet
- mercury, called "quicksilver"
- mirrors
- bells

Magellan meets the King of Cebu. Magellan later renamed Cebu and the surrounding group of islands the Philippines, after Prince Philip of Spain.

The End of the Journey

Magellan should have saved his tears. The worst part of the voyage was still to come!

Magellan's Last Stand

Magellan had no idea how big the Pacific Ocean was. He thought he could cross it in two or three days. The voyage took about four months! The crew began to starve. They ate insects, rats, sawdust, and the leather strips from the sails. By the time they reached the island of Guam and fresh food supplies, many sailors had died from an illness called scurvy.

The ships sailed on to the island of Cebu (part of the present-day Philippines), where the islanders gave the men shelter and more food. Magellan became friends with the king of Cebu and converted him to Christianity. In return, Magellan agreed to help the king fight his enemy on another island. On April 27, 1521, Magellan was killed in battle.

Magellan thought that his men would easily defeat the islanders. He was wrong.

What Is Scurvy?

Scurvy is an illness due to a lack of vitamin C caused by not eating fresh fruits and vegetables. Many sailors became sick with scurvy on long sea voyages when their limited supplies of fresh food ran out or went bad. The symptoms of scurvy are painful. Victims suffer from blackened, bleeding gums, and their teeth fall out. They also have aching limbs and joints, and sores that spread all over the body. In the end they die from bleeding inside the body.

Finding the Spice Islands

After Magellan died, there were only enough men left to crew two ships. So they burned the ship that was in the poorest condition. In November 1521, the two ships finally reached the Spice Islands. They loaded up with spices, silks, and pearls.

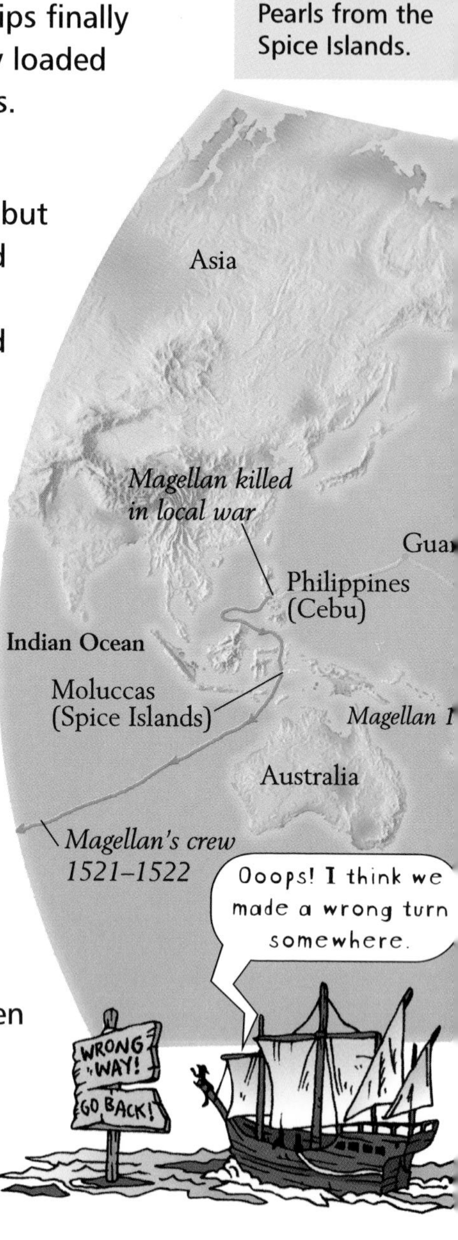

Pearls from the Spice Islands.

Back at the Beginning

The *Victoria* headed for Spain, but the *Trinidad* had to stay behind for repairs. By the time it was seaworthy, the ship had missed the favorable seasonal winds. Its crew decided to sail east across the Pacific, but the Trinidad was later captured by the Portuguese. But on September 8, 1522, people in southern Spain were surprised to see a shabby, leaking *Victoria* sail into the harbor. On board were just 18 of the 270 men who had set sail three years earlier.

Magellan had died, but his voyage had achieved the unthinkable. The globe had been **circumnavigated** and the way opened for more exploration.

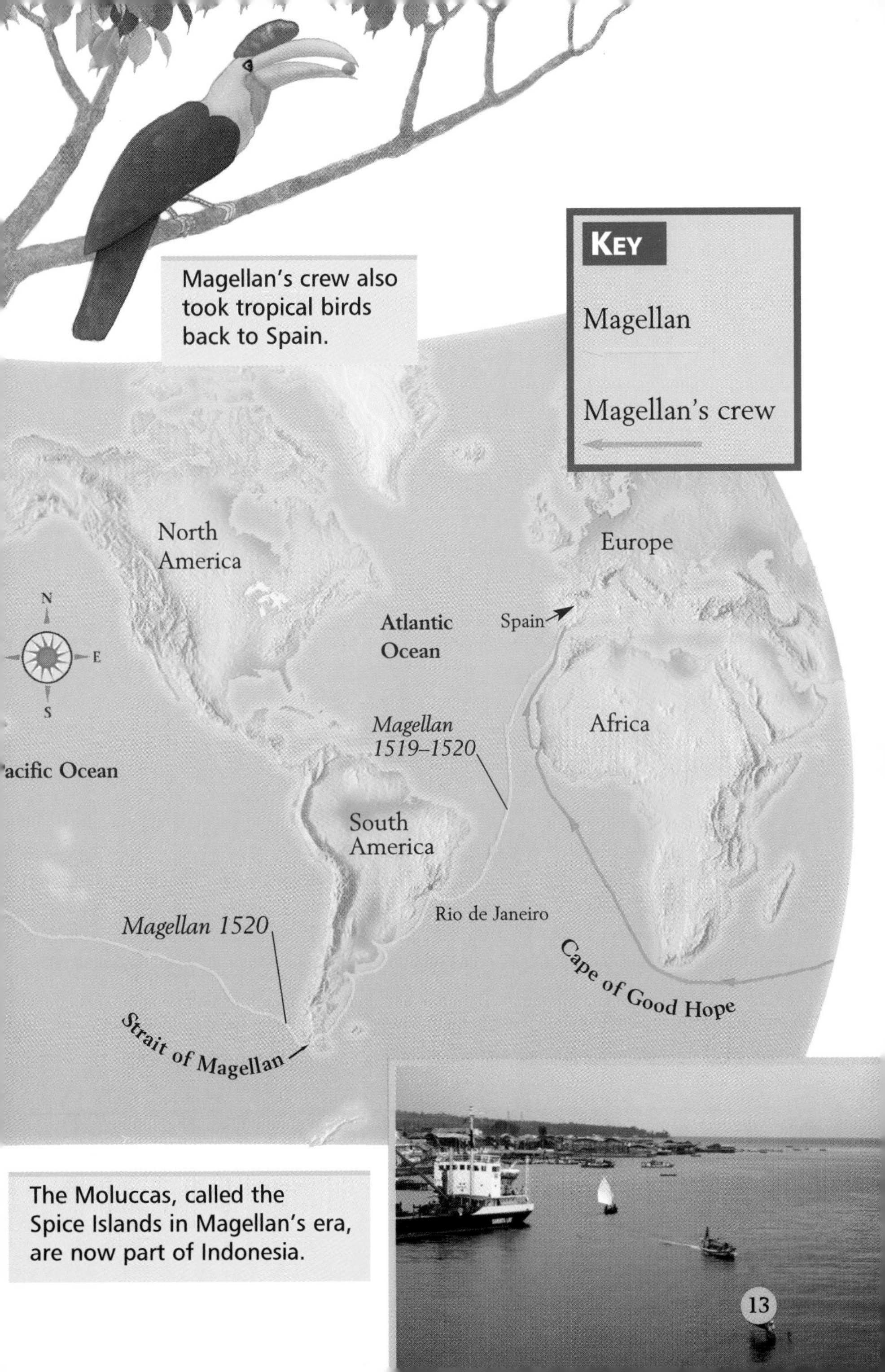
Magellan's crew also took tropical birds back to Spain.
KEY
Magellan
Magellan's crew
North America
Europe
N
E
S
Atlantic Ocean
Spain
Africa
Magellan 1519–1520
acific Ocean
South America
Rio de Janeiro
Magellan 1520
Cape of Good Hope
Strait of Magellan
The Moluccas, called the Spice Islands in Magellan's era, are now part of Indonesia.

VOTES
FOR
WOMEN
VOTING
SHOULD BE
FOR EVERYONE
EN

Fighting the Good Fight: Emmeline Pankhurst

She fought as bravely as any soldier to win her war!

Some trailblazers sail into the unknown in search of wealth and glory. Others, like Emmeline Pankhurst, a champion of women's rights, come from the most unlikely backgrounds.

Emmeline was born in Manchester, England, in 1858. It was a time when women were supposed to have only one role—looking after the home. But Emmeline saw a different role for herself. Even at a young age, she was interested in advancing the rights of women. Her husband, Richard Pankhurst, was sympathetic to her cause until he died in 1898.

The Fighting Spirit

Although she was raising four children alone, Emmeline was still determined to fight for the right of women to vote.

All for One

In 1903, Emmeline formed the Women's Social and Political Union (WSPU) to campaign for women's **suffrage**—their right to vote. She believed that having the vote would give women the chance to bring about other much-needed changes in society.

Emmeline Pankhurst speaking at a meeting.

Emmeline (third from right) and her daughter Christabel Pankhurst (second from left) with friends.

In the beginning, Emmeline's followers used peaceful methods of marches, meetings, and appeals to politicians. But none of the political parties supported or even cared about the issue. Emmeline knew she needed to bring attention to her cause. She and her followers, called **suffragists**, began a **campaign** of disobedience. They knew that this would get them into the newspapers.

The WSPU logo. The WSPU was the first organization to use buttons, badges, and medals.

Soldiers in Skirts

The suffragists shouted at politicians and threw flour bombs. They chained themselves to railings outside, and to benches and grilles inside, the Parliament. They threw rocks through windows and used acid to burn the words "Votes for Women" into golf courses. During these demonstrations and protests, many of the suffragists were physically battered.

A suffragist chained to a grille inside Parliament.

Lawbreakers to Lawmakers

Emmeline and the suffragists were laying the foundations for change. Through their courage and willingness to suffer for their beliefs, they forwarded their cause.

Death of a Foot Soldier

In 1913, one of the suffragists became a **martyr,** dying for her cause. Emily Davison tried to grab the reins of the king's horse during a race. She was trampled and died four days later. Her funeral was one of the biggest suffragist demonstrations ever.

The British Houses of Parliament.

Emily Davison's funeral. Emmeline was not there. She was arrested as soon as she stepped out of her house to attend.

Prisoners of War

Many suffragists were arrested. They all chose to go to prison rather than to pay a fine. Once in prison, the women would go on a **hunger strike**. After several days of this, they were usually force-fed. This was very painful, and it gained them much sympathy from the public.

What Is Force-Feeding?

The prison wardens tried to tempt hunger strikers with tasty food. This usually failed, so then they reached for tubes and funnels. Three or four strong wardens held the woman down, while a doctor pushed a rubber tube down her throat into her stomach. A form of liquid food was then poured into the tube. This made the woman vomit again and again. The ongoing cycle of hunger, force-feeding, and vomiting ruined the health of many suffragists.

Emmeline Pankhurst being arrested. At her trial, she said, "I look upon myself as a prisoner of war."

Women and the Vote

Some countries were faster than others to give women the vote.

1893 — New Zealand

1902 — Australia (except Victoria in 1908)

1906 — Finland

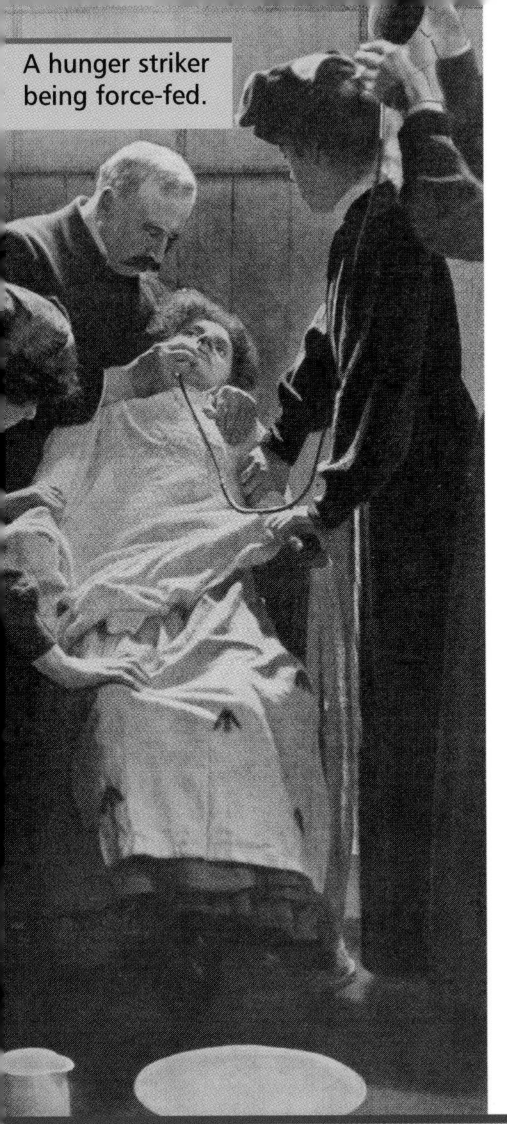
A hunger striker being force-fed.

Times of Change

World War I broke out in 1914. People, including Emmeline, were concerned with the need to win a war. She joined in helping with the war effort. During the war, women did many of the jobs that men had done before. Four years later, Britain emerged as one of the winners of a long, bloody war. But society had been changed forever. Now that women had worked alongside men, more people accepted the idea that women should be allowed to vote. In 1918 women over the age of 30 in England were granted the right to vote. Emmeline had won her war, too.

- 1913 — Norway
- 1915 — Denmark, Iceland
- 1917 — Russia
- 1918 — Austria, Hungary, Poland, Germany, England (for women over 30 years)
- 1919 — Netherlands
- 1920 — United States, Czechoslovakia
- 1921 — Sweden
- 1928 — England (for women over 21 years)

Breaking Down Barriers: Nelson Mandela

He spent a total of 27 years in prison in order to be free in his own country.

Nelson Mandela was a quiet man. But the cruel and harsh treatment of people of color by South Africa's white government leaders forced him to speak out.

In South Africa, black people and other people of color made up the majority of the population. But they were not allowed to vote and were forced to live in crowded, rundown areas. They could only get low-paying, and often dangerous jobs that white people would not do. Every day they lived under this unjust system that was designed to keep them separate and not at all equal.

Changing Ways

Nelson Mandela knew that it was time for change. But it would be a long road to freedom.

Born to Be Free

Nelson Mandela was born on July 18, 1918. His father was a leader in the Thembu tribe, so the young Nelson went to meetings of tribal elders. When he was twelve, his father died, and the Thembu king, Chief David Dalindyebo, adopted him. The dignity Nelson always showed may have come from this experience of growing up in the traditional culture of his **ancestors**.

Black South Africans had to carry a pass at all times. Here, Nelson Mandela is about to burn his pass in protest.

At school and while he was studying law, Nelson met other people who knew that the conditions in South Africa were wrong. He joined a group called the African National Congress (ANC). The ANC was based on the nonviolent resistance taught by Mahatma Gandhi of India. The ANC opposed the **apartheid** laws that denied black people most of the rights that white people had.

The house where Nelson Mandela was born, in Transkei in the Eastern Cape of South Africa.

This is a house shop in South Africa in 1946. Conditions for many people of color there have not changed.

Nelson Mandela's tiny cell. When he lay down he could feel one wall with his feet, while his head grazed the opposite wall.

The Terrible Years

The 1950s and 1960s were violent years in South Africa. There were riots and **strikes** by black people and armed **reprisals** by the government. Many men, women, and children died. Nelson organized protests and **boycotts**, and the government "banned" him. This meant he could only talk to one person at a time, and he could not attend public meetings or speak to other banned people. But Nelson continued to protest and was arrested many times. In 1964, he was sentenced to life in prison and was sent to Robben Island with other political prisoners.

In 1960, 69 unarmed native South Africans were killed in Sharpeville, South Africa. Police opened fire on a group protesting the rule that non-whites had to carry a pass.

From Prisoner to President

Being in prison did not stop Nelson Mandela's fight for freedom.

Prison Rules

There were very strict rules at the maximum security prison on Robben Island. Prisoners were allowed only two letters and two visits a year, and they were not allowed to read newspapers. Scraps of information passed secretly from cell to cell as the men tried to get news of the outside world.

Prisoners had to get up at 5:30 AM every day to work in a lime quarry. Here, they are crushing stone in the prison yard.

The Slow Walk Home

To the prisoners it seemed that time had stopped. But in South Africa and across the world their families and friends were keeping their cause alive. Pressure was growing for these prisoners and all South African people of color to be given the same rights enjoyed by whites. In 1985, the South African government offered Nelson his freedom. But there were strings attached. He would have to give up all struggle and opposition to the government. He chose to remain a prisoner.

The world watched as Nelson Mandela, surrounded by his wife and supporters, finally left prison.

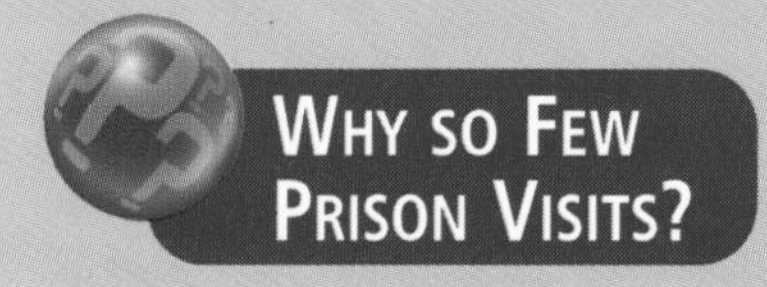

Why so Few Prison Visits?

Nelson was allowed to see his wife twice a year. But the government made these visits nearly impossible. Forced to take an expensive flight part of the way, his wife also had to endure questioning and sign piles of documents. Then she had to ride in a ferry's cargo hold to Robben Island, where she was often still turned away. The couple sometimes went two years between visits.

The Nobel medal for peace

In February 1990, Nelson Mandela was finally released without conditions. Crowds of people blocked the gates and roads, and millions watched on television as this now elderly man proudly walked free.

In 1994, South Africa held its first one-person, one-vote elections. When the votes were counted, South Africa had its first black president—Nelson Mandela.

Nelson Mandela casts his vote in the 1994 election.

In 1993, Nelson Mandela and F. W. de Klerk, then president of South Africa, shared the Nobel Peace Prize for their efforts to end apartheid.

Vision, courage, and determination can achieve great things.

Timeline of Other Barrier Breakers

Birth/ Death	Name	Nationality	What He/She Achieved
c.551–479 BC	Confucius	Chinese	His philosophical sayings and views on life became the basis of Chinese religion and society.
c.1254–1324	Marco Polo	Italian	His travels through China and the East brought back new knowledge and skills to Europe.
1780–1845	Elizabeth Fry	English	She set up schools for children in prisons and worked to improve the terrible conditions in jails.
1820–1910	Florence Nightingale	English	Her work as a nurse led to much-needed improvements in hospital standards.
c.1821–1913	Harriet Tubman	American	She was born a slave, but she helped hundreds of other slaves escape to freedom.
1869–1948	Mahatma Gandhi	Indian	His method of peaceful disobedience and nonviolent protest won independence from Britain for India.
1880–1968	Helen Keller	American	Although blind and deaf, she learned to read, write, and speak, and she became an inspiration to millions.

Note: c. is an abbreviation of *circa,* which means "about."

Glossary

ancestors a person's relatives in the distant past

apartheid the name, meaning "separateness," of the system in South Africa that kept black people away from white people

boycott to stop buying or using something as a form of protest

campaign a course of activities for a specific purpose

circumnavigated sailed around

hunger strike refusal to eat as a form of protest

marooned put ashore on a deserted island or coast as a punishment or as a result of a shipwreck

martyr someone who willingly suffers death for a belief or cause

mutiny to revolt against or disobey those in command

reprisals acts of revenge that cause similar or greater injury to an enemy

strait a narrow passage of water connecting two larger bodies of water

strike to stop work or activities in order to protest the actions of employers or governments

suffrage the right to vote

suffragists women who were members of an organization that supported women's suffrage

marooned

Index